Alchemy
Workbook

by Dennis William Hauck

- ♦ **Alchemical Mandalas**
- ♦ **Symbolic Engravings**
- ♦ **Meditation Exercises**
- ♦ **The Emerald Formula**

Athanor Books

ISBN 0-9637914-4-3
AlchemyStudy.com

OUTLINE of the WORK

Introduction

This workbook is intended as an experiential guide to the ancient art of alchemy. The principles revealed here are based on many centuries of alchemical practice and date back to a time when some of the most creative minds in the world delved into the intertwined mysteries of matter and energy, soul and spirit. Those philosophers of nature sought universal laws of transformation that were as valid in their laboratory experiments as they were in their own hearts and minds. Their legacy to us is an amazing spiritual technology that works on all levels at once, a powerful Science of Soul whose principles are as valid in the physical world as they are in the psychological and spiritual realms.

The alchemical philosophers got their inspiration from a single document called the Emerald Tablet. It is said to have originated not with mortal men but with mysterious godlike visitors who arrived in Egypt over 12,000 years ago. Ancient Egyptian scrolls referred to them as the "Group of Nine" and credit one of them named "Thoth" (the God of Thought) with teaching mankind writing and mathematics. Just before the Great Flood, Thoth preserved the visitors' teachings in a time capsule of wisdom sealed within a great pillar. The pillar survived the flood and when opened was found to contain many scientific manuscripts, as well as the wondrous Emerald Tablet. The crystal tablet's smooth bas-relief lettering spelled out a succinct summary of the ancient wisdom and carried with it a powerful gift for the future evolution of mankind. Encoded within the tablet's words was a secret formula for transforming reality!

The secret formula in the Emerald Tablet became the basis for the discipline of alchemy. Medieval alchemists had copies of the tablet hanging on their laboratory wall and constantly referred to the hidden formula it contained. To hide the true nature of their Work from power-hungry monarchs and medieval churchmen, each step of the formula was described in chemical terms. But though the alchemists spoke of furnaces, flasks, and beakers, they were really talking about changes taking place in their own bodies, minds, and souls.

"The Emerald Tablet is the cryptic epitome of the alchemical opus," says Jungian analyst Dr. Edward Edinger, "a recipe for the second creation of the world." "Whatever one chooses to believe about it," notes John Matthews in *The Western Way* (Penguin 1997), "there is no getting away from the fact that the Emerald Tablet is one of the most profound and important documents to have come down to us. It has been said more than once that it contains the sum of all knowledge — for those able to understand it." Like other explorers of consciousness, Terence McKenna recognizes that the Emerald Tablet contains "a formula for a holographic matrix" that is mirrored in the human mind and offers mankind its only hope for future survival.

Each of the seven steps in the "Emerald Formula" are presented and elaborated in the following chapters. There are also relevant engravings and drawings that the alchemists actually used to activate the corresponding steps within themselves. These drawings are actually alchemical mandalas, whose deeper meaning can be absorbed only through repeated meditation. By following the suggested exercises and meditating on the drawings included here, you can initiate alchemy within yourself and begin your own personal transformation from the lead of your everyday self into the gold of a perfected spirit living in accord with the higher laws of the universe.

▽ Calcination

Chemical Calcination

In order to transform something, it must first be reduced to its most fundamental ingredients. All the dross, falsity, and extraneous material must be removed. It is the job of the first two operations in the Emerald Formula to see that this purification is done correctly and completely. After these two operations of Fire and Water, the essences of the matter at hand should be readily available to be separated out of the remaining "dark matter."

The alchemists called the initial Fire operation in the Work during the purification process "Calcination," which means literally "reduced to bone" by burning. In the laboratory, Calcination is the heating of a substance an intense flame until all that is left is a pile of white ashes. Often the substance is pulverized using a mortar and pestle and then heated over an open flame in a crucible. The alchemical symbol for Calcination is the crucible (▽).

Psychological and Spiritual Calcination

Ever felt as if everything was going wrong in your life no matter what you did? Ever have days when whatever you attempted seemed to backfire on you? You have experienced the fires of Calcination. As strange as it seems, your quality of consciousness or inner attitude have a lot to do with how life treats you, with what kind of "justice" comes your way on a daily basis. A leaden consciousness attracts lead in your life and invites the fires of hell; a golden consciousness attracts gold in your life and invites the light of heaven to shine down on you.

Psychologically, Calcination is the destruction of the leaden center of consciousness, which is the ego and all the illusions and self-deceptions it maintains to protect or enshrine itself. Personal Calcination means getting free of the stranglehold of earthbound ego and replacing it with the true Self, which is rooted on a higher or golden plane of reality. For most of us, Calcination is a natural humbling process as we are gradually assaulted and overcome by the trials and tribulations of life. People caught up in Calcination often feel as if

they are trapped in the fires of Hell, burning up and suffering through their life yet unable to escape. Surprisingly, it is not until these fires are burning that your transformation begins, for the only way out of Hell is rise up with the flames. Fortunately, controlled Calcination can also be achieved. It begins with a deliberate surrender of our inherent *hubris* (pride or vanity) through a variety of spiritual disciplines that ignite the fire of introspection and self-evaluation. "Its father is the Sun" says the tablet of this first step in alchemy.

Before undergoing Calcination, people are stubborn, materialistic, and fearful of change. About the only positive quality that can be found in such a person is a certain practicality born from having their dreams repeatedly squashed. However, those who have passed through Calcination no longer approach the world through the pulpit of the calcified ego, for they have discovered a higher more "fluid" identity at the tabernacle of soul. People describe being in the presence of a calcined person as "refreshing." They sense the freedom of no longer having to be manipulated or controlled by deceits of someone else's ego.

Working in the Inner Laboratory

Where does the fire for deliberate personal Calcination come from? It is the same flame from which the light of consciousness emanates. The Secret Fire of the alchemists is concentrated consciousness. If you cannot concentrate or focus your mind, you simply cannot do alchemy. Alchemy is nothing but the purification and concentration of consciousness. During this first step in transformation, you have to turn up the fire of consciousness and concentrate it on your thoughts, habits, assumptions, and judgments. You have to be utterly truthful about all situations, all relationships. In this way, you learn to recognize falsity and burn away the leaden or crystallized thoughts that often take on a mind of their own and become unintended responses or robotic reactions to people and events. During Calcination, you use the fire of consciousness to burn through illusion, self-deception, defense mechanisms, bigotry, and all the other dogmas and dramas of the Tyrant Ego who has usurped the throne of the transpersonal Self who is the rightful ruler of the personality. As in the Grail legend, the kingdom of your personality will wither and decay until the King is restored.

For many centuries human beings have been engaging in an activity that is designed specifically to get beyond the illusions of ego and contact the essence of Self. Meditation is the art of focusing concentration and directing your attention inward, without regard to the demands of the external world, in order to move beyond ego and achieve union with your spiritual core. "All things have come from this One Thing," says the Emerald Tablet, "through the meditation of One Mind." That One Mind is the same for everyone, and it can be found in meditation.

However, alchemistic meditation is different from other forms, because it is an *active* instead of a passive discipline. The alchemist's meditation seeks to actually *work* with the transcendental powers beyond ego to create something new. The object is not to still the mind but to fill it with images and follow those images back to their divine source. Obviously, the most important component of this type of meditation is the power of imagination, what the alchemists called True Imagination. They understood True Imagination to be the ability to create meaningful images in the mind, as opposed to fantasy, which means insubstantial daydreaming. True Imagination is the evocation of inner images which does not spin groundless fantasies but tries to portray them true to their archetypal nature.

Experiment 1: Pulverizing Ego

Let's begin our work in the Inner Laboratory by trying to crush ego. Truly, this is not an easy task. Most people have built their entire lives around the desires and demands of their ego. Yet, for each of us there have been moments of utter humiliation in which ego has been at least momentarily defeated. Think back to one of these experiences in your own life and use that energy to try to free yourself from the control of ego. Think back. Did someone ever really embarrass you? Did you ever make a wrong decision that caused pain or havoc for others? Were you ever caught performing some act you were not supposed to be doing? Did anyone ever blame you for something bad happening? How did you feel

at these moments when your ego was deflated or defeated? Don't rationalize! Remember ego is constantly rewriting history to portray itself in a better light. Bring back those events and feelings as vividly and completely as you can. They have great power to put your ego in its place and expose the falsity of the world it supports. After awhile, you should be able to just remember what it felt like to have a crushed ego and perpetuate that state of consciousness for use in the next phases of your alchemy. Personal ego and the superego of society are the greatest threats to personal transformation. You have to get beyond them to really change yourself.

Experiment 2: Roasting Cinnabar Meditation

A Calcination exercise that allows you to get in touch with your True Imagination is a meditation session called "Roasting Cinnabar." Cinnabar is a naturally occurring mineral, a brilliant red sulfide of mercury that Chinese alchemists called "Dragon's Blood." If the rocks are roasted over an open flame, drops of pure mercury ooze from the crevices and fall into the ashes with heavy thuds. If cinnabar is ground up and heated in a glass container, the mercury condenses on the side of the glass like a mirror.

For these reasons, the ancients considered cinnabar a magical mineral, and early alchemists were convinced they had discovered the elusive First Matter during the Calcination of cinnabar rocks. The elemental mercury produced by roasting cinnabar has all the characteristics of what the alchemists thought the First Matter should look like. It has the heavy, watery qualities of the One Thing from which the universe was created, and like the primal chaos of creation, mercury has no form of its own. In fact, Mercury is the only metal that is liquid at room temperature, and because other metals liquefy at higher temperatures, mercury was though to possess the soul of all metals and is their precursor.

The object of the Roasting Cinnabar Meditation is to probe the hardened red mass of reactionary judgments and buried emotions that are hidden but still responsible for much of our behavior. The hardened cinnabar rock represents your ego. The meditation begins by entering a relaxed state, in which you divorce yourself from the strivings and concerns of everyday life. Start out sitting in a comfortable chair or laying propped-up by cushions on a bed or couch. We are going to use deep, rhythmic breathing to entrain the body and mind into a relaxed state. Slowly count back from ten, and with each count, take a slower and fuller breath while progressively relaxing every part of the body starting with the toes and working up to the scalp muscles.

Once you are totally relaxed, try to visualize the bright red cinnabar roasting over a blazing fire. Think back over your life to the times you were uncontrollably angry or deeply frustrated or utterly embarrassed. Try to dredge up the thoughts and feelings that were experienced then because they are directly tied to your ego's sense of control. Those experiences are still there hidden inside the red rock, because your ego buried them there. You know you are getting close if you start to feel uncomfortable or upset. It may be necessary to turn up the heat and gather all your willpower to stay focused on these inglorious memories, but there is a reason.

In the meditative state, you are temporarily divorced from ego and can clearly see the follies and injustices of ego-centered existence. You will quickly discover that the ego is entirely a reactive device designed to perpetuate the illusion of itself. Perhaps you loved someone who did not love you back, or you tried to help someone and only ended up making things worse, or you hurt a beloved pet or a close friend out of anger. Maybe someone took advantage of you or made a fool of you. We all have had such denigrating experiences, and sometimes because of them, we "get burned" and silently promise never to let those things happen again. Our egos go to extreme lengths to get even or to never allow the opportunity for such things to take place again. The alchemists saw those hardened thoughts as "metals" within us and believed they made up our temperament.

However, those searing thoughts are our part of the energy that drives our lives, and if we bury them, we surrender life force. Those ignoble thoughts become part of our behavior, encrusted patterns of response that turn us into ego-driven zombies. There is no simple formula like "from now on I will be more loving" or "starting Monday I will be more open with my coworkers." That type of planning and goal setting is the hallmark of ego. All we can do is become aware of our hidden assumptions and everyday thoughts and witness how we turn control of our lives over to the most insubstantial part within us.

After working through one or two or these egotistic memories, keep the fires of introspection burning and try to hold onto the original thoughts while visualizing the hot mercury seeping out of the roasting cinnabar. Don't let go of those thoughts as you visualize yourself catching the mercury with a glass bottle as it oozes from the rocks. What you are holding is the fabled genie-in-a-bottle, the power of liquefied, free-flowing thought. This is the power of pure consciousness, still warm to the touch and uncontaminated by ego. During the higher stages of alchemy, you use it to get anything you want by refashioning it into the directed light of the living imagination.

Experiment 3: Bodily Calcination

As with all the operations in alchemy, Calcination takes place not only on the psychological and spiritual levels but also within the body itself. Not surprisingly, your ego also perpetuates a false notion of your body as something beautiful and eternal. But take a good look in the mirror! Your body is nothing but a 72-year-long chemical reaction, and your metabolism is the calcining fire that will consume it. About the only noble thing that comes out of your blossoming into physical reality is the consciousness you carry. According to many traditions, that consciousness is distilled many, many times – until we get it right, until we make it incorruptible and golden. In alchemical terms, your body is the vehicle of your transformation.

Bodily Calcination uses aerobic exercises to fan the fires of metabolism. Jogging, biking, swimming, or just rapid breathing in a sitting position, use the lungs like a bellows. The result is a biological purification and elimination of toxins, and a concentration of life force in the body. Mindful physical exercise is a powerful tool in personal transformation if performed with a positive attitude. The body is not only the temple of the soul, it can become a sacred talisman to remind us that alchemy is real and works on levels.

Many times bodily alchemy is expressed as a "second puberty," a rebirth into a more youthful and healthy state. This accounts for the numerous reports of alchemists living for hundreds of years. We will continue to examine the effects of bodily alchemy in the following chapters.

℧ Dissolution

Chemical Dissolution

The second step in the purification process is dissolving the ashes from Calcination in water or acid. The ashes disappear, as if it they have returned to their original, undifferentiated state, and the alchemists saw this as a return to innocence, a return to the womb for rebirth. The symbol for Dissolution is the womblike retort (℧).

Psychological and Spiritual Dissolution

By middle age, many people feel they have lost a precious part of themselves and are leading inauthentic and superficial lives. Our souls despair trying to survive in a world of spiritual drought, and we have less psychic energy available. The purpose of psychological Dissolution is to dissolve rigid beliefs and any remains of ego falsity the hold back the powerful "waters" of the subconscious mind. Tremendous energy can be generated when the waters held back are released, as the ego is humbled by his direct confrontation with the primal energies of the unconscious.

"Its mother is the Moon," is how the tablet describes this second step in the Emerald Formula. Just as Fire is the element of the Sun, so is Water the element of the Moon. During Dissolution, the lunar powers expressed in dreams, visions, psychic impressions, and bodily feelings take precedence over the linear approach of the rational mind. Successful Dissolution requires letting go of control, allowing feelings to flow, and repressed thoughts and feelings to surface. You might be overwhelmed by images, wordless impressions, and strange feelings, and feel like you are really floating around aimlessly in a giant sea, but this is only a temporary process in the long road to renewal and perfection.

Undissolved people are judgmental, greedy, and excessive, and their relationships can only be described as selfish. In such persons, the process of Dissolution results in a withdrawal of projections and judgments and a breakdown of assumptions and habits resulting in a wonderfully flowing, childlike presence. The person is no longer afraid to express that which is within. The result is a release of pent-up energy previously spent supporting the false personality.

Experiment 4: The Bain Marie Meditation

Jewish alchemist Maria Prophetissa invented a method of Dissolution that became the standard process for washing the remains of Calcination. Called the "Bain Marie," it is basically a double-boiler in which the water in the bathing vessel is kept at a constant temperature by immersing it in a second container of water being heated.

Besides its practical application, the Bain Marie is also a useful meditative tool for handling the destroyed psychic remains resulting from Calcination. The Bain Marie Meditation exudes a maternal warmth, and the fire of consciousness is turned down considerably. The idea is to dissolve or melt away the burnt-out thoughts and emotions dredged up during the previous blaze of introspection and treat them as a cohesive whole.

Seated or lying down, calm yourself with several deep breaths, and then inhale very slowly. Imagine you are taking in the warm, dissolving waters of the Bain Marie with each breath. Hold the breath and let it "work" those painful emotions or on any area in your body where you feel tension or pain. Then exhale slowly and deeply, as deep as you can, and imagine those hardened, hurtful areas melting away. Repeat this circulation of dissolving "waters" as long as it takes until you feel genuine relief. Then relax and breath normally. If you feel the troublesome areas in your body or mind returning, begin the Bain Marie again. Remarkable results can be obtained with this very basic exercise in just a few sessions.

The time required for this visualization to work depends on how deep and crystallized your psychic energy has become. What will it take to dissolve you? Ask yourself in what ways have you been hurt by unrequited love or another person's wrath. Was someone mean to you, or did someone abuse you? How did you react? Relive the experience, but this time, work with it. Your wound is your gold and in order to mine the precious metal within, you have to be willing to relive your pain. That means not thinking about the individual incidents behind emotions but rather trying to feel and work with only their pure energy or "vital principle." If you can dissolve the connections between emotions and their source, the energy will be free to use for transformation.

Experiment 5: Cibation

Another relevant exercise at this stage is the Cibation Meditation. It is based on a technique in alchemy called Cibation, which is the addition of water or other fluids to the dried-out matter at the precisely the right moment to complete its Dissolution. Psychologically, this is a sensitizing process in which painful memories or hardened reactions are dredged up and felt again with the goal of refining the emotions behind them. In this type of meditation, we examine the areas of our psyche that appear the driest and most crystallized, then we "add" emotional energy to re-experience them again with the objective of breaking them down.

Usually it is at this point that you rediscover your pain and can release the energy of crystallization by liquefying it and making it flow again under your control. So, go back to your childhood and retrieve the most painful memory you can find. Re-experience the day a loved one died — a pet or friend or relative — and cry until you can cry no more. You must make yourself cry for Cibation to occur, so do not be afraid to feel the pain again. Medieval alchemists believed that the salt in tears represented remnants of crystallized feelings and thoughts broken down by crying. This crying technique has proved successful over and over again in treating eating disorders, sex problems, drug abuse, depression, insomnia, and anger, and it is one of the fastest working methods in all of psychology.

Experiment 6: Dreamwork

Since dreams carry the power of Dissolution, it is necessary to learn to work with dreams to open up new creativity, make new connections, and restructure old habits. Dreams carry important subconscious knowledge about health, life events, and relationships that the ego refuses to acknowledge. Carl Jung first became interested in alchemy when he noticed the wealth of alchemical imagery in the dreams of his patients.

To start paying attention to dreams, you have to treat them as important information. Most people have dozens of dreams every night full of insight and meaning but forget them on awakening. Very quickly on rising from sleep, the ego takes control with its endless planning, scheming, and judgments. Unless a recurring dream or nightmare disturbs this habitual pattern, most people do not remember their dreams.

So the first step in dreamwork is to accumulate dream material. Keep a notepad or tape recorder by the side of your bed to summarize dreams from which you awake in the middle of the night. In the morning, get into the habit of laying in bed awake for a few minutes trying to remember dreams you had. Start a dream journal with your own interpretations, then compare the symbolism with the dreams of your friends or use any of the numerous dream interpretation books available. Just keep in mind that dreams are very personal information about what is happening in *your* life and not all images have the same meaning for everyone. You have to interpret dreams in context with your current situation, feelings, and stage of transformation.

Experiment 7: Bodily Dissolution

One of the most powerful methods for dissolving the body is fasting, and it has long been part of many religious disciplines. Not only does fasting purge the body of toxins and the effects of overindulgence, but it activates a healing response from the body. Most animals respond to illness by seeking solitude and refusing to eat, and fasting has also been used to treat a variety of diseases, including such common illnesses as cancer, diabetes, tuberculosis, high blood pressure, and schizophrenia. The psychospiritual benefits of fasting are numerous. It clears the mind, refreshes the memory, and opens to mystical experiences.

Fasting is a way of becoming stronger by letting go — a kind of proactive denial of worldly temptations. Start with juice fasts for a single day or over the weekend. Try to notice how not eating affects your mind and body. The more toxins that have built up in your body and mind, the more uncomfortable are the first efforts at fasting. It is important to drink plenty of water so the toxins can be easily flushed from the body. Alchemical fasts continue for three to thirty days and should only be undertaken in a spiritually relaxing environment. Fasting is a great time to practice Calcination and Dissolution techniques and melt away mental and physical blockages to the soul.

✧⊸ SEPARATION

Chemical Separation

Separation is the isolation of the desired components from the previous two purification operations (Calcination and Dissolution). In the laboratory, the components of the polluted solution from Dissolution are separated out by filtration, cutting, settling, or agitation with air. Any ingenuine or unworthy material is then discarded. The alchemical symbol for Separation is a stylized cipher representing the process of filtration (✧⊸).

Psychological and Spiritual Separation

If performed correctly, the operations of Fire and Water described in the previous two chapters have revealed the most basic constituents of the matter at hand. Now it is the job of the life-bringing element of Air to isolate and invigorate the material worthy of further attention. "The Wind carries it in its belly," says the Emerald Tablet of this phase. The alchemists saw this as an impregnation of the personality with something entirely new, as our true essences come alive and shine through the murky waters of Dissolution.

In psychological terms, Separation is when you lift yourself out of the quagmire of your broken ego personality and recognize your unborn self. By breaking down yourself into your most basic traits and desires, you become aware of the essences within and isolate them from ego complexes and unwanted unconscious elements. Personal Separation is the discovery of your individual essences and the reclaiming of dream and visionary "gold" previously rejected by the masculine, rational part of your mind. You review formerly hidden material and decide what to discard and what to reintegrate into your refined personality. Much of this shadowy material are things we are ashamed of or were taught to hide away by our parents, churches, and schooling. Separation is getting beyond restraints to your true nature, so the real you can shine through.

People who have not yet begun the process of Separation can be overly assertive and controlling, refusing to compromise in even the most mundane matters. At their worst, they are driven by frustration and anger and can become cruel or violent. On the other hand, people undergoing Separation are courageous and daring, often initiating major changes in the world and in the lives of the people around them.

Experiment 8: Sifting Identity

A wide variety of psychological Sifting Techniques are available for the alchemist to cut through worldly illusion and catch the ego in its deceptive habits and manipulations. A method called "Sifting Identity" is a private meditation in which you simply relax, concentrate on your breath, and periodically ask yourself the question "Who is aware?" In the silence of the response, you can feel your own consciousness at the very ground of your being. Alternatively, sit in a silent, dark room and repeat your name to yourself over and over, trying to determine what it really means. By observing yourself observing yourself, you enter an infinite progression or mental loop — until finally there is no difference between you the observer and you the observed, between you and your own consciousness. That primal awareness is a big part of your true identity, your true Self. Out of the intense focusing of your consciousness on yourself, your individuality fades away into a boundless realm and is replaced by something so vast and eternal that death itself seems a laughable impossibility. During Separation you realize that the loss of personality is not extinction but the only true life.

Experiment 9: Cutting Through Reality

The object of this exercise is to cut away all but the purest essences of everything around you. It is what alchemists called dealing only with the "true signatures" of every person, thing, event, or situation. The sword you use to cut through reality is your own consciousness honed to penetrate even the deepest illusion. You sharpen this sword of knowing by living on the *edge* between this world and the next, between matter and mind, between life and death. You no longer immerse yourself totally in the everyday world. The way in which we pay attention to the everyday world is called the First Attention, and most people only know this single way of relating to the world. Yet it is possible to open the doors to a another reality, parallel and separate from normal reality. If you look at someone with your First Attention, you see a person's body and physical attributes and usually make some kind of judgment based on that information. However, if you defer judgment and use the Second Attention, you can sense things about their character, deepest secrets, and even state of health.

Shamans spend many years developing the Second Attention, though they usually begin by simply focusing on things that normally go unnoticed. Concentrating on shadows instead of objects, focusing on a person's body movements rather than what he or she says, or simply doing something routine in a different way (like walking backwards) are all first steps in this process. By entering a state of "not doing" or not participating in this world by living on the edge between worlds, and halting the internal dialogue that supports the First Attention, the shaman heightens his intuitive awareness of reality and eventually develops Second Attention.

Experiment 10: Alchemistic Aeration

Aside from psychological techniques, there are a number of physical methods for bodily Separation. Some of these methods date back over 3,500 years to Egyptian alchemists who taught spiritual breathing techniques in the city of Akhetaton. These methods centered on working with the subtle life force that, according to the Emerald Tablet, the Wind "carries in its belly." Known in Indian alchemy as "prana" and in Taoist alchemy as "chi," this vital breath is responsible for a person's state of health and can also be harnessed for his or her psychospiritual transformation.

Most of us would agree on examining our breathing rhythms that they are related to mental states. Emotions of fear, love, and embarrassment all cause changes in our breathing, as does boredom, inspiration, calmness and other intellectual qualities, and many actors have learned how to turn emotions on and off by eliciting the appropriate breathing pattern. Whether they are aware of it or not, public speakers, hypnotists, psychics, and healers, all exercise some control over pranic forces. Alchemistic Aeration directs and stores the

vital breath within 0the body so it can be used by the spiritual seeker. The goal is to become "Thrice Greatest" at breathing and manifest life force on all three levels of the lungs. Most of us have fallen into the habit of breathing on only one level, thus depriving themselves of vital energy. The stomach breather fills the lower part of the lungs; the rib breather, who uses only the intercostal muscles of the ribs, fills the pulmonary midsection with air; the top breather, who raises the shoulders and collarbones when taking in air, fills only the uppermost portion of the lungs. When exhaling, most people squeeze out only the top of the lungs, causing stagnation of the tiny air sacs in the lungs and limiting the amount of fresh air that can be taken in.

The ideal breather aerates the entire lung cavity on every breath and empties it completely during exhalation. To try this yourself, sit upright in a chair and relax. Using the diaphragm, take a deep breath while expanding the stomach, followed by a slow expansion of the rib cavity, and culminating in upper-lung breathing that can be felt all the way into the throat. Then exhale completely, starting at the base of the lungs and climaxing at the top. Exhalation should take twice as long as inhalation. For example, practice inhaling for a count of eight and exhaling for a count of sixteen, while concentrating on filling and emptying all three levels of the lungs.

To begin Alchemistic Aeration, follow the above breathing pattern but pause for a count of twenty-four after inhaling. At first it may not be easy to break years of improper breathing habits, but keep practicing until you are able to achieve these minimum periods of inhalation, retention, and exhalation. They can be expanded in the proportion of three counts of holding the breath and two counts of exhalation for every one count of inhalation. The purpose of this exercise is to allow the breath to follow mind and establish a conscious connection between the two.

It is in the pause between breaths that many experience something more profound than just physiological breathing. While holding the breath, some practitioners feel an involuntary rhythm rise in their bodies that brings a fluid energy to the core of their being, and they feel as if they can go on holding their breath forever. This experience is known as embryonic breathing or the Primordial Breath, a sensation of breathing without breathing that puts them in direct contact with the subtle essence of the life force that we all have within us.

☿ CONJUNCTION

Chemical Conjunction

If the preceding three operations were successful, only the most genuine and essential parts of the matter are left in the vessel of transformation. The next step is the Conjunction, which is the recombination of those saved elements into a new substance. In general terms, Conjunction is the paradoxical union of the archetypal elements of Fire, Water, and Air to produce Earth. The symbol for Conjunction (☿) is a stylized cipher representing the union of opposing compounds or essences to produce an entirely new thing.

Psychological and Spiritual Conjunction

Psychological Conjunction is the empowerment of our true selves, the union of both the masculine and feminine sides of our personalities into a new belief system or state of consciousness. The alchemists referred to the result of the Conjunction as the "Lesser Stone," and after it is achieved, the adept is able to clearly discern what needs to be done to achieve lasting enlightenment. Often, synchronicities begin to occur that confirm the alchemist is on the right track. In spiritual terms, these essences are the very soul and spirit of the alchemist, and it is now time for the feminine and masculine essences to come together and nurture their newborn child. "Its nurse is the Earth," says the tablet of this important juncture.

Before Conjunction, a person can be lustful and wanton in seeking their "other half" and jealous and possessive once it is found. On the other hand, the conjuncted person is appreciative of the alchemical forces at work in relationships and careers, and tends to be considerably kinder and more sensitive. Such a person appears balanced and quietly confident, and that inner harmony is proof of the integration of the elements within.

Experiment 11: Creating the Overself

The goal of this exercise is to integrate the masculine and feminine ways of knowing into a unified and more powerful whole within the personality of the alchemist. This Conjunction of opposites creates an "Overself" in which the ways of spirit and soul (rational thought and intuitive feeling) unite in a higher state of awareness Egyptian alchemists called "Intelligence of the Heart." The work here is done in the everyday world, and it is not necessary to enter a meditative state.

To create the Overself, you simply have to start practicing to maintain your "presence" no matter what happens, no matter how confusing things get, no matter what emotions swell up within you, no matter how cruel or thoughtless others are towards you. Every problem, every personal challenge, every nuisance or annoying person, is another opportunity for you to develop presence of mind and create the Overself. In trying to maintain your "presence" in all situations, you soon learn that you cannot rely on intellect or logic alone. To be really connected to what is real, you have to make use of talents and sources of knowledge that you cannot explain. Finally, you learn to value your feelings and intuitions as well as your rational judgments.

Do not forget that these two opposing ways of knowing only come together when they are *used* together. You have to practice personal Conjunction on a daily basis in the "real" world for the Overself to become part of your personality. The major effort in the alchemist's life is the creation of this unified self, which can withstand the onslaughts of ignorance, insensitivity, and illusion one encounters in the world. You actually can feel yourself coming together as one mind, one larger presence. Signs that Conjunction is taking place within a person are the growth of confidence, equanimity, and calmness. You start grinning at stupidity instead of getting angry. Within you, the feeling of an indestructible or "default" presence grows stronger every day. That personal presence is what the alchemists called the "Lesser Stone," which will gradually be perfected and emerge as an all-powerful state of consciousness they referred to as the "Greater Stone."

Experiment 12: Earth Alchemy Meditation

Shamans work with the Four Elements in much the same way as alchemists. In the parlance of Native Americans, working with the Earth element is "Earth Medicine," and sacred power spots are marked with rock formations that align with the rising sun. Shamans connect with the powers of the Above and Below by accessing the One Thing, what Sioux medicine men call the "limen" or "place where the power moves freely, untransformed." After journeying to this realm and mastering the powers of the Other Side, the shaman returns to share his visions and energy.

You can tap into the powers of the planet by communing with nature regularly, but to reach deep enough to resonate with the life force within you requires deliberate concentration. One approach for working with these powers is the Earth Alchemy Meditation, which interprets the four cardinal directions as archetypal pathways that define not only our location in space but also our location psychologically and spiritually. In this scheme, the balanced center (or Overself) can be accessed from any of the four directions. It does not matter what path one takes as long as one arrives at the center, where the masculine and feminine in you are balanced and the transcendent qualities of spirit and soul can be united.

In a field or forest clearing, find a central location and mark it with a circle of rocks or use a natural marker such as a tree stump or boulder. Sit down cross-legged facing north. Now, relax and contemplate each of the four directions as manifestations of the Four Elements, both within you and on the planet. Spend ten or fifteen minutes reflecting on the following qualities of each direction and then turn clockwise to face the next direction. Make the like elements resonate between you and the outdoor environment.

According to Native American myth, the polar or north direction is associated with the Earth Element. It is home to the powers Below: night, winter, the hidden sun, the fallen moon, ancestors, ancient wisdom, and physical sensation. It is also home to sacred horned animals, such as the reindeer and the white buffalo, and even creatures like the unicorn. Looking to the north, try to feel the archetypal Earth, the powers of manifestation and matter, and what it would be like to be a wild animal surviving in this untamed environment.

Next, turn eastward in the direction of the Air Element. It is home to the rising sun, spring, birth, thought, and new beginnings. Out of the golden sky of the east comes the soaring eagle. Try to feel the optimism of the dawn and the freedom and perspective of the eagle. Listen to the Wind.

Then, turn to the south or equatorial direction, home of the Fire Element. This is the direction of the noon sun, summer, childhood, passion, spirit, and the masculine powers. The archetype of the noontime sun is embodied in animal totems that include family or den-oriented animals like wolves, coyotes, and mountain lions, as well as domesticated animals like dogs and cats. Re-experience the warmth of the home fires and the innocence of childhood as you face the source of Fire. Try to touch this archetypal Fire.

Now turn to face the west, home of the Water Element. Since the moon appears brightest after the setting of the sun, native cultures connect the lunar presence with the west. The western horizon is the direction of the sunset, fall, maturity, harmony, soul, deep feelings, and the feminine powers. Its totems are ocean-born mammals such as the dolphin and whale or hibernating animals like bears. Try to be very still while looking west and open yourself to its unconscious, intuitive wisdom. Pay close attention to any signs of Water.

Finally, return to the facing-north position, but this time, try to feel all the varied energies of the different directions at once. Let them come together within you. This is not a thinking process, so you have to open yourself up and let the elements flow into you and harmonize with the like elements within you. Like our planet itself, you too are made up of Fire, Air, Earth, and Water. Like the planet, you too are alive with yet a Fifth Element. This is at the central spot you created, the one-point where all Four Elements come together to create the Quintessence or the Overself, the one person that you really are.

Experiment 13: Bodily Conjunction

That the human body must be perfected, as well as the mind and spirit, is a basic tenet of alchemy. Yet how do King and Queen manifest in the body, and what exactly is the Child of the Conjunction in terms of human physiology?

According to Tantric alchemists, the phallic-shaped pineal gland at the center of the brain and the bilobed pituitary gland play the roles of King and Queen. Their union, which is achieved through meditative exercises, produces a Pill of Immortality, which is released at the back of the throat and is activated when it reaches the stomach. This inner sex act initiates a Second Puberty that perfects and rejuvenates the body.

FERMENTATION

Chemical Fermentation

Chemical Fermentation is a natural process consisting of two parts. First comes Putrefaction, in which the matter is allowed to rot and decompose. The alchemists even added manure to help get the process going. The sign that Putrefaction is nearing its end is a milky white fluid that accumulates on the blackened, rotting material.

The dead material seems to come to life again with an influx of digesting bacteria, as Fermentation begins. This new life force changes the fundamental nature of the material in what the alchemists saw as a process of spiritization. Out of the utter blackness of Putrefaction comes the yellow Ferment, which appears like a golden wax flowing out of the foul matter. Its arrival is announced by the formation of an iridescent, oily film the alchemists named the "Peacock's Tail."

Psychological and Spiritual Fermentation

Psychological Fermentation is the introduction of new life into the personal presence (or Overself) that developed during Conjunction. This Child of the Conjunction, however, is really just a gross melding of opposites that may still be contaminated with traces of ego, so it is necessary to "sacrifice" it to bring about its resurrection on a new level of being. During psychological death or Putrefaction, the Child of the Conjunction, which is the strongest presence you can create within your earthbound personality, is exposed to the decadent humidity of your deepest and most clinging psychic components, the psychological manure in which most of us wallow.

This is the dark night of the soul, in which you realize how futile it can be to try to overcome the personal, social, genetic, and even astrological limitations to change. The enthusiasm of the Conjunction turns into a black mood, and there is an extinction of interest in life. At this point, you have to stubbornly persist to achieve enlightenment or relax into the dull slumber of mere physical existence. Like the white light of the Other Side seen by near-death experiencers, we finally leave the darkness and enter the bright light of resurrection as consciousness is restored on a higher level.

Fermentation starts with the inspiration of spiritual power from Above that reanimates, energizes, and enlightens the blackened soul. It can be achieved through various activities that include intense prayer, desire for mystical union, breakdown of the personality, transpersonal therapy, psychedelic drugs, and deep meditation. In simplest terms, Fermentation is a living, loving inspiration from something totally beyond us, something existing wholly Above in the realm of pure mind. "Separate the Earth from Fire, the Subtle from the Gross" the Emerald Tablet instructs us at this stage.

Like the iridescent "Peacock's Tail" of its chemical counterpart, successful psychological Fermentation is indicated by colorful visions that symbolize the activation of the True Imagination — what the alchemists called their "Secret Fire." Personal awareness and creative abilities skyrocket in this state of consciousness, and Fermentation is the quality we envy in great artists, prophets, and spiritual leaders. Once fermented, a person becomes suddenly alive and irrepressibly hopeful because their attention is diverted from this world to something much greater.

Experiment 14: Capturing the Fermental Light

Like the fires that burn constantly in the alchemist's laboratory, the Secret Fire becomes the alchemist's primary tool during the higher stages of the Great Work. The light of the Secret Fire experienced in mystical visions, meaningful dreams, near-death and out-of-body experiences, paranormal encounters, and with psychedelic drugs, is, surprisingly, the same. That Fermental Light is always close at hand and only the veil of our assumptions of materiality needs to be lifted to see it. Let's do a very simple experiment in personal Fermentation.

First, sit back in a comfortable chair, fold your hands in your lap and relax; then, close your eyes and concentrate on the first image that pops into your mind. Do not be concerned if it is some-thing you had just seen or if there is no image at at all. Give it a little time and allow that image, or pattern, or blankness, or whatever, to change and grow. Pay attention to the morphing image and try to remember as many details about the scene as you can. Now, ask yourself a question — something you really want to know — and see what happens. Observe how the image alters itself and what the final version looks like. Open your eyes again. Simply report to yourself what you saw in as much detail as you can remember.

If you visualized someone from the office lying naked on your waterbed, you have probably missed the point. The idea is not to engage our fantasies but to allow images to rise on their own from an unconscious source. This is True Imagination of which the alchemists spoke. Try it again at a later time if your images are being driven by wish-fulfillment or from instincts such as visions of a juicy hamburger if you have missed lunch. The curse of modern man is that he confuses fantasy for the amazing power of True Imagination and thus relegates both to the psychic trash heap.

However, during this little experiment, you might have seen something that you had not previously noticed or something that an independent part of your mind was still dwelling on. You might have seen something unexpected or allowed the image to become fluid and were able to communicate with that independent part. In such instances, you need to interpret what was seen and how it changed when you asked your question.

The fluid light you experienced is the same Fermental Light that emanates from the Secret Fire within all of us, and this internal vision quest can be expanded to become a significant part of your life. If you work at it, it can put you in contact with a deeply truthful intelligence within yourself that you never knew existed. In fact, the alchemists measured a person's mental health by the degree to which imagery was used — by how well nourished was his or her imagination.

Experiment 15: Bodily Fermentation

Bodily changes begun during Conjunction reach an entirely new level during Fermentation. The Second Puberty of Conjunction causes the growth of a Second Body, a body of light first experienced only in the True Imagination.

During the initial stages of personal Fermentation, the level of inspiration can become so intense that it is experienced as a palpable warm light circulating in the body. This living inspiration can even be consciously directed as a healing energy to various parts of the body or to others. As Fermentation progresses, people report feelings of extraordinary grace and "flow" as the physical body raises toward perfection, toward an ideal or archetypal image that is slowly taking on reality within.

DISTILLATION

Chemical Distillation

Chemical Distillation is the boiling and condensation of a solution to increase its concentration and purity. The alchemists believed that Distillation released the essence or "spirit" of a substance. For instance, the spirit wine is produced by distilling a solution of fermented grapes.

The alchemical symbol for Distillation (Δ) is the alembic, which is a hood that fits over the boiling fluid, condensing the rising vapors, and directing the purified condensate via a funnel or tube to a collecting vessel. Repeated Distillation produces an extremely concentrated solution the alchemists called the "Mother of the Stone."

Psychological and Spiritual Distillation

In psychological terms, Distillation is a repeated separation and recombination of the subtle and gross aspects of the personality. This agitation and sublimation of psychic forces is necessary to ensure that no impurities from the inflated ego or submerged id are incorporated into the next and final stage of transformation. To make sure that no traces of imperfection remain, the product of Fermentation must undergo repeated Distillation before it can be reborn permanently on a higher level. "It rises from Earth to Heaven and descends again to Earth" says the tablet of this distilling process.

The process continues until peace and wellbeing on all levels bond to the personality. Psychological Distillation consists of a variety of introspective techniques that raise the content of the psyche to the highest level possible, free from sentimentality and emotions, cut off even from one's personal identity.

Spiritually, Distillation is the purification of the unborn Self — all that we truly are and can be. Distillation is a rejuvenating immersion in the womb of the primordial forces of the universe that marks the final death of ego and the birth of the transpersonal Self.

Undistilled people are still subject to emotional extremes and influenced by the forces of lust and greed. Once distilled, however, a person gains astonishing equanimity and unflappable one-pointedness. Distilled persons become highly intuitive and undeniably psychic when they take the larger view to which they are privy.

Experiment 16: Circulating the Light

Chinese alchemists became proficient at spiritual Distillation thousands of years ago. In a discipline called "Circulation of the Light," the aspirant is taught to concentrate on the light of the inmost region and, while doing so, to free himself from all outer and inner entanglements. During the first stage of this Distillation, Mercurial or watery consciousness is used, and the light is gathered by quieting the body and mind through breath awareness and meditation. The fermental light of the True Imagination is a kind of seed energy scattered throughout the body, and the object is to bring it all together in a vessel, such as a retort or oven, visualized in the abdominal cavity just below the navel.

In the second phase of the Circulation of the Light, Sulfuric or fiery consciousness is used to initiate the movement of the accumulated light energy. With concentration fixed at the level of the abdominal vessel, the practitioner wills and feels the light circulate up the "channel of function" through the chest cavity to the "precious cauldron" at the center of the brain. There, the light energy is distilled and accumulated, and any unconverted energy returns to the navel area via the "channel of control" that runs down the back along the spine.

The adept repeats the Circulation of the Light daily for months or even years, until enough of the "light" collects to crystallize in the cauldron within the brain. According to Chinese alchemists, the subtle matter distilled through this process congeals into a Golden Pill, which is the adept's passage to perfect health and even immortality.

Experiment 17: Bodily Distillation

There are many "moving meditations" that

are designed to accomplish Distillation of the life force in the body. The slow and graceful movements of the ancient art of Tai Chi Chuan are designed to make the practitioner aware of the subtle light energy (chi) as it circulates in the body. The sadhana postures of kundalini yoga actually attempt to bind one's awareness to this energy, so it can be followed upward as it is distilled from the body in a union of the individual's consciousness with the infinite consciousness of God. People actually feel as if they are rising up into the Above and returning again to earth. In some instances, physical levitation is reported, which is another sign of successful bodily Distillation. All these exercises work with the vertical axis in the human body, which is the Hermetic caduceus or ladder of transformation along which the seven steps in the Emerald Formula are visualized as chakras — knots of energy that are untied or lotus flowers that bloom as the energy rises during Distillation.

♌ COAGULATION

Chemical Coagulation

Chemical Coagulation is the precipitation or sublimation of the purified Ferment from Distillation. In alchemical metallurgy, the baser metals are transformed into incorruptible gold during this stage. The symbol for Coagulation (♌) is a stylized cipher depicting the permanent union or fusion of opposites.

Psychological and Spiritual Coagulation

Personal Coagulation is first sensed as a new confidence that is beyond all things. Coagulation incarnates and releases the "Ultima Materia" of the soul, which the alchemists also referred to it as the Greater Stone. Using this magical touchstone, the alchemists believed they could create an Elixir that would cure all diseases and heal all wounds on all levels.

During Coagulation, the body is made spiritual and the spirit is made corporeal. Coagulation thus transcends both heaven and earth and produces a new incarnation that can survive in both realms. On the personal level, this manifests as an out-of-body experience — the creation of a Second Body, the Golden Body of light, a permanent vehicle of encapsulated consciousness that embodies the highest evolution of mind.

Just before the final Coagulation occurs in people, they might appear to be self-involved due to their preoccupation with finding divinity within. Afterwards, they exude a unique higher Presence, a steady confidence in their daily activities, and others begin to see them as authentic and whole persons whom they want to emulate. People sense the divine Presence and sometimes want to worship it, not realizing it is just an example of what they can themselves become.

Experiment 18: The Grand Meditation

The Emerald Tablet promises that during Coagulation "you will you obtain the Glory of the Whole Universe; all Obscurity will be clear to you." However, during this operation, we must endure the same kind of existential torture that God (the One Mind) went through to manifest from the One Thing, which is the background reality that is present in both nonexistence and existence, both sleep and waking, both death and life. The creation of the Second Body is almost a corollary to this primary act of creation, since the birth of new consciousness requires embodiment.

The way to Coagulation of spirit is shown to us step-by-step in the Emerald Formula, and during the Grand Meditation, we attempt to recreate this process in one sitting. As we have seen, the seven operations in this formula are: Calcination, Dissolution, Separation, Conjunction, Fermentation, Distillation, and Coagulation. Ideally, the aspirant should memorize the Emerald Tablet and repeat it during this meditation. Alternatively, the seven steps can be followed in the order they are presented in the tablet. During the initial transformation of consciousness, we use the first three steps to disentangle ourselves from the manifest world and isolate our purest essences, then we pull these essences together in a purified incarnation or presence in the fourth step (Conjunction). During the final transformation, we apply the next three steps to reassemble the purified essences of our being on the highest level.

To begin the Grand Meditation, take a comfortable position in a quiet place, where you will not be disturbed. The best time to practice this meditation is in the morning or after taking a short nap. Begin by closing your eyes and breathing in very deep, slow breaths, then progressively relax your muscles, starting at the at the tips of your toes and moving upward until you reach the back of your head. The technique is to relax and observe your current thoughts, emotions, and bodily tensions and notice any involuntary changes in breathing as you examine each area. If you feel tension in your breathing, it is a sign that you need to work on that area or subject matter until it is resolved. If your mental contents are tied to concerns about work, friends, or family, you have to break free of the world and align yourself with the vertical axis of reality connecting the Above and the Below.

This initial realignment requires the use of the methods you have already learned to achieve personal Calcination and Dissolution. You must become free of egocentric striving, petty feelings, and body blockages, to get in touch with your truest and deepest essences. This is not the time, however, to dredge up old feelings and ideas. During the Grand Meditation, you deal only with the base material of the day, as you attempt to transform your current temperament. Using the Fire of your introspective consciousness, try to overcome the established parameters of your psyche and burn away the hold your ego has on you. Similarly, by allowing the Water of your unconscious contents to rise, experience your hidden side and try to understand how it is responsible for much of your behavior. Do not proceed from Calcination and Dissolution until you really believe you have exposed ego and have gotten beyond its illusions, and your body is fully relaxed. Clues that this is happening are a feeling of numbness in the muscles, a blank mind, and a clear visual field.

In the next phase, Separation, relax your ego and body to the point where neither are active. Try to keep a gentle awareness of what is going on, while you put your body and brain to sleep. This condition of relaxation coupled with awareness is known as the hypnagogic state. It may take some practice to achieve, but it is the gateway to experiencing the One Mind. Continue in this state for awhile and simply let go of any spurious images or thoughts that arise. Try to enter an even deeper state of relaxation and try to exist only within your mind. Relax so much that you loose all bodily awareness and sensory input shuts down. Become what the alchemists would describe as "hermetically sealed."

At this point, you exist in a void where the only source of stimulation is your own thoughts. You are literally existing within the Secret Fire, and your thoughts have tremendous power here. You can intensify this separated state even further by identifying with the strongest currents or forces in this environment. These purified forces come from your own soul and spirit, and they may appear as energy patterns or alchemical images. These normally opposing forces in your personality can be united easily in this non-rational environment by applying the power of thought. Simply picture it and make it so in a new Conjunction. What you have created is the Child of the Philosophers.

Your conjuncted identity is a center of consciousness that has been described in many spiritual traditions. The Hindu one-point (or bindu), is the center of the cosmic axis and represents the turning point of existence into non-existence. For the Chinese, the indefinable singularity known as the Tao is the source of all things, while Buddhists seek to follow the Middle Path back to the center of the creator. In Conjunction, you reach a plateau that the alchemists called the Lesser Stone. In this state of mind, you have broken free of personal and social restraints to the expression of your true Self.

To break through to the Above and achieve the higher alchemy, the Emerald Tablet tells us to "Separate the Earth from Fire." It means to remove all matter, including base emotions and ego, from the Secret Fire of imagination. Having purified and isolated the subtle components of our being, we set up a kind of sympathetic correspondence with the very real and living powers of the Above. In the Grand Meditation, this is experienced as a sense of vibration originating just overhead, and it is a direct confrontation with the higher frequencies of the light spectrum. This is something real that has been documented in several scientific collaborations between psychologists and physicists that concluded the archetypal or divine energy exists as psychoid (mental and physical at the same time) factors located in the invisible ultraviolet end of the spectrum in the area of high energy cosmic rays. This lends further credence to the idea that alchemical transmutation occurs at the level of the spirit but causes repercussions in the physical realm as well.

Try to bring these real higher vibrations down into your body during the Fermentation phase of the Grand Meditation. Pull them into the top of your head and push them down into your physical frame. Feel them surge throughout your whole body. Concentrate on entraining yourself to the wave pattern entering your body from Above. Make these divine frequencies vibrate in you from head to toe. Now, follow these waves as they travel back up and out of your body; then stay with them as they come back down and reenter you. Keep this circulation going until every fiber of your being is in tune with these vibrations. At this point, you are beginning to experience "dematerialization" in the alchemical sense. During this Distillation or spiritizing phase, your physical body is the Ferment, the subtle womb from which your Second Body will emerge.

Experiment 19: Coagulation of a Second Body

After becoming proficient at the Grand Meditation, proceed to the final step in transformation. Follow each step of the Grand Meditation, then extend the Distillation process as long as you can. As the rising and falling waves of Distillation continue, try to observe how the vibrations disperse in your body and then coalesce to depart from your body. During Coagulation, you must gain control of this vibrational state and start to crystallize the subtle energy into a Stone — your truly independent Second Body.

Begin the birth of this body gradually, by extending a hand or foot beyond your physical frame. Increase the limb's vibrational rate if necessary, then touch some object near you. Push your hand or foot right through it; realize that you are not in a totally physical state anymore. Now, return your limb to coincide with your physical body and relax the vibrational rate. For most people, this is enough for the first time. Reduce the vibrations in your body and let the two bodies merge. Lie still as your physical body returns to normal.

When you are committed to travel completely out of your body, go through the seven steps of transformation until you are deeply entrained in the vibrational state. Feel your entire body vibrating and then start to roll, unfold, or lift yourself out of your body. Some people can simply jump free all at once. While performing this disassociation with your body, think about how lightweight you are becoming. Truly desire to exist outside the body and dismiss any extraneous thoughts. You must use all your willpower now. Feel yourself becoming lighter and lighter and think how wonderful it would be to exist in a subtle body. Fear will pull you back into the body, so try to understand that nothing can harm you during the birth of your Second Body.

You are still connected to your body by the golden umbilical, whether you can see it or not. Start by exploring the room you are in, and next time, travel through your entire apartment or home. Try to notice objects that will confirm to you that you are really out of your body. You are beginning a journey in which the places you can visit are endless. All you have to do is think about

them and you are there. After you experience the freedom of this boundless body, you can verify the words of the Emerald Tablet yourself: "This is the greatest Force of all powers, because it overcomes every Subtle thing and penetrates every Solid thing."

The Three Magisteriums

Be patient in the practice of the Grand Meditation and ultimate Coagulation. The alchemists believed that ultimate success came in three broad stages they called "magisteriums," to which they gave the names of different Stones. During the First Magisterium, the Lunar Stone is created. It represents gaining control over the body, so that every fiber and tissue can be completely relaxed. The Second Magisterium, the Solar Stone, is achieved when the mind is controlled through willpower, so that fear and ego do not interfere. The Third Magisterium is the union of the Lunar and Solar Stones with the cosmic presence to create the Stellar Stone or Astral Body.

Seen another way, the Conjunction is the union of the Lunar Stone with the Solar Stone, the Marriage of the King and Queen, to create the Lesser Stone in which we become centered and gain control over mind and body. Coagulation, then, is the union of the Lesser Stone with the powers Above to create the Greater Stone of the Golden or Astral Body. Having achieved that Greater Stone, you have broken free of genetic, environmental, and astrological restraints to your being and are free to express the bliss of your true Presence — your personal Stone.

At this stage, you are born into the universe and have arrived at a new plateau, the Greater Mysteries of the ancients. This is true atonement with the mind of God, and it allows you to enter the "graduate school" of spiritual instruction where you learn to exist within the Whole Universe — both the seen and unseen, manifested and unmanifested. However, getting into "heaven" is not the final stage in alchemy. There is really an eighth step in the Emerald Formula, a step off the ladder of transformation and a return to where we started. "Its inherent Strength is perfected," we are told, "if it is turned into Earth." Successful Coagulation is only made real if it "descends again to Earth" and continues in the alchemical processes of Projection and Multiplication to perfect others and all matter. In this view, we are truly the "salt of the earth."

The Emerald Formula

The Octave of Creation

The alchemists believed the tablet contained the formula for transforming everything — not only physical matter but the subtle substances of mind and spirit as well. They realized that the Emerald Tablet offered a time-tested formula that actually *works* with something we perceive as metaphysical in nature and thus presents a true Spiritual Technology for the human race.

As we have learned, the Emerald Formula consists of seven consecutive operations of transformation, which are Calcination, Dissolution, Separation, Conjunction, Fermentation, Distillation, and Coagulation. Like the musical octave, the Emerald Formula is composed of seven "vibrations" of consciousness that when completed lead to an entirely new vibration or state of consciousness that becomes the first note of a still higher octave. Each octave is a higher division of consciousness that penetrates higher dimensions of reality. This Music of the Spheres is the evolution of Mind in the universe. Just like the "do-re-mi-fa-so-la-ti-do" of the musical scale, the "notes" or steps of the Emerald Formula have the same basic relationship within each octave. In the words of the Emerald Tablet, the notes Below "correspond" to the notes Above, and the notes Above "correspond" to the notes Below. In this way, the universe is one flowing, beautiful composition in the Mind of God.

Experiment 20: The Azoth Mandala

To guide us through a deeper understanding of the Emerald Formula, we are going to make use of a tool actually used by the alchemists, a meditative emblem first published in 1659 as an illustration for the book *Azoth of the Philosophers* by the legendary German alchemist Basil Valentine. The word "Azoth" in the title is one of the more arcane names for the One Thing. The "A" and "Z" in the word relate to the Greek alpha and omega, the beginning and end of all things. The

word is meant to embrace the full meaning of the One Thing, which is both the chaotic First Matter at the beginning of the Great Work and the perfected Stone at its conclusion.

At the center of this striking drawing (see next page) is the face of a bearded alchemist at the beginning of the Work. Like looking into a mirror, this is where the adept fixes his or her attention to begin meditation. Within the downward-pointing triangle super-imposed over the face of the alchemist is the goal of the Work, the divine man in which the forces from Above and Below have come together. The alchemist's schematized body is the offspring of the marriage between Sol, the archetypal Sun King seated on a lion on a hill to his right, and Luna, the archetypal Moon Queen seated on a great fish to his left. "Its father is the Sun," says the tablet, "its mother the Moon."

The jolly, extroverted Sun King holds a scepter and a shield indicating his authority and strength over the rational, visible world, but the fiery dragon of his rejected unconscious waits in a cave beneath him ready to attack should he grow too arrogant. The melancholy, introverted Moon Queen holds the reins to a great fish, symbolizing her control of those same hidden forces that threaten the King, and behind her is a chaff of wheat, which stands for her connection to fertility and growth. The bow and arrow she cradles in her left arm symbolize the wounds of the heart and body she accepts as part of her existence.

In simplest terms, the King and Queen represent the raw materials of our experience — our thoughts and feelings — with which the alchemist works. The King symbolizes the power of thought, ultimately the One Mind of the highest spirit. The Queen stands for the influence of feelings and emotions, which are ultimately the chaotic One Thing of the greater soul. The much anticipated Marriage of the King and Queen produces a state of consciousness best described as a feeling intellect, which can be raised and purified to produce a state of perfect intuition, a direct gnosis of reality. The goal of alchemy is to make

this golden moment permanent in a state of consciousness called the Greater Stone, and it all starts with the marriage of opposites within us, which they thought of as the Lesser Stone.

In our drawing, the body of the alchemist is composed of the Four Elements. His feet protrude from behind the central emblem; one is on Earth and the other in Water. In his right hand is a torch of Fire and in his left a feather, symbolizing Air. Between his legs dangles the Cubic Stone labeled with the word *Corpus*, meaning body. The five stars surrounding it indicate that it also contains the hidden Fifth Element, the invisible Quintessence whose "inherent strength is perfected if it is turned

into Earth." Where the head of the alchemist should be, there is a strange winged caricature that is variously interpreted as a heart, a helmet, or the pineal gland at the center of the brain. This represents the Ascended Essence, the essence of the soul raised to the highest level in the body, to the brain, where it becomes a mobile center of consciousness able to travel outside the body.

Touching the wings of the Ascended Essence are a salamander engulfed in flames on the left side of the drawing and a standing bird on the right. Below the salamander is the inscription *Anima* (Soul); below the bird is the inscription *Spiritus* (Spirit). The salamander, as a symbol of soul, is attracted to and exposed in the blazing fire of the Sun. Likewise, the bird of spirit is attracted to the coolness of the Moon and is reflected in it. This is a subtle statement of the fundamental bipolar energies that drive the alchemy of transformation. *Spiritus*, *Anima*, and *Corpus* form a large inverted triangle that stands behind the central emblem. Together they symbolize the three archetypal celestial forces that the alchemists termed Sulfur, Mercury, and Salt. Again, these chemicals are not chemicals at all, but our feelings, thoughts, and body.

Step One: Calcination (▽)

Now you can begin working through the seven stages of transformation in the drawing. The hidden matter with which you are going to work is the One Thing within you, your soul, which the great alchemist Paracelsus referred to as the "Star in Man." This secret star is depicted as rays that spin out from the alchemist at the center of the mandala. The shaded ray shooting downward to the Cubic Stone is labeled number one and represents both the beginning and end of the Great Work. This ray is also marked with the cipher that stands for both the metal lead and the planet Saturn. Saturn is the Ancient One, Old Man Time with his scythe and crutch. But Saturn is crippled for a reason: he is the slowest planet, and his metal, lead, is heavy and dull. Together they symbolize the inertia and weight of the soul which produce the stubborn, materialistic, and melancholic temperament of the leaden person. We all know such people from Saturn. In their relationships with others, they tend to be passive-aggressive, smart-alecky, and like to keep others waiting, but they can also be extremely loyal and family-oriented. What the saturnic personality needs most is a fire lit under them — a calcining flame to initiate their transformation.

Nearest the alchemist in this shaded ray is the square symbol for Salt. The ancients associated Salt with thinking because of its property of crystallization. They believed thought was a living substance made of moving images that crystallized into beliefs and assumptions in the mind of man. Thus, Salt in the initial stages of alchemy represented stifled or lowered consciousness, which when raised through the seven steps, dissolved and recrystallized into a higher form. This breakdown in crystallized thought (or altering of belief systems) is the primary objective of the

first two operations of alchemy. The release through the eyes of dissolved salt in tears signified that alchemical processes really broke down thoughts and feelings in man.

Moving clockwise in the drawing, we come to the first of seven circles containing scenes depicting the operations of alchemy. The first circle (located between the first and second rays) shows a black crow perching on top of a skull. Below it on the outer ring is inscribed the Latin word *Visita*, meaning to visit or start a journey. This circle depicts the Soul Bird during the process of Calcination, in which everything lower has been burnt away. In chemical Calcination, a substance is heated over an open flame or in a crucible until it is reduced to ashes, and this is the first application of the Fire Element in the tablet. In psychological terms, this is known as the Death of the Profane, an operation on the saturnine elements of the personality that results in the death of ego and extinction of interest in the material world, as the soul realizes the illusions it has embraced. Calcination is the destruction of ego and all its defense mechanisms. These mechanisms usually take the form of self-perpetuating delusions and attachments to appearances and material possessions. In the worst case, a person's basest instincts are constellated in his or her psyche and given power over the entire personality. In such instances, a person must endure the most horrendous hellfire that eventually reduces his or her life to shambles. Therefore, the intensity of the calcining fires varies between individuals, though Calcination always represents the beginning of a Black Stage in our lives when we are reduced to our most basic components. For most of us, Calcination is a natural process that takes place over time, as we are gradually assaulted and overcome by the trials and tribulations of life. But for the alchemists, Calcination is a controlled burn achieved by a deliberate surrender of our materiality through a variety of spiritual disciplines that ignite the passion in our souls. In all these instances, Calcination is working with Fire to burn away artificial constructs and reveal a person's true essence.

Step Two: Dissolution (♌)

The second ray of the Azoth of the Philosophers points toward the King's domain and is marked with the symbol that stands for both the metal tin and the planet Jupiter. This ray is white or light gray in color. The person with a tinny temperament relies on his or her own judgment to guide them, although their assessments tend to be based on outer appearances. This reliance on intellectual processes produces a practical, superficial, and tin-like temperament. In relationships, the person from Jupiter is likely to be motivated by strictly physical cravings or monetary gain yet can also be a good provider for others. What the jupiterean needs most is to be submerged in the waters of Dissolution to gain true depth and perspective on the deeper levels of reality.

The second circle depicts the black Soul Bird watching itself undergoing Dissolution, literally dissolving before its eyes in the powerful forces of the unconscious. This internal Water takes the form of dreams, voices, visions, and strange feelings which reveal a less ordered and less rational world existing simultaneously with our everyday life. Reflecting back from the pool of Dissolution is the white image of the essence of the Soul Bird, which is exposed during this operation. In the outer ring next to the circle of Dissolution is the word *Interiora*, meaning the interior or innermost parts, the source of our emotions and feelings.

Psychologically, Calcination is the further breaking down of the artificial structures of the psyche by immersion in the unconscious or the "irrational" and rejected parts of our minds. "Its mother is the Moon" says the tablet, referring to the activation of lunar consciousness at this stage and the first application of the Water Element described in the tablet. Just as Calcination works on the mind and ego to destroy deceptions and impure thoughts, so does Dissolution work on the heart and id to release buried emotions that conceal or distort our true nature. It is, for the most part, an unconscious process in which our conscious mind allows the surfacing of previously buried material. Dissolution is working with the Water Element by opening our personal floodgates and generating new energy. It results in a wonderfully flowing presence that is free of inhibitions, prejudgments, and restrictive mental structures. That which is within us is now close to the surface and freely expressed.

Step Three: Separation (◊⟶)

The third ray of the Azoth points toward the torch of Fire and is marked with the cipher signifying both the metal iron and the planet Mars.

This ray is colored red and is also marked with a smaller symbol denoting Sulfur. The iron individual is a willful, aggressive, and hot-tempered person, whose actions are dominated by a conquering energy that turns everything toward him or herself. Sulfur stands for the masculine, active force being expressed here. In relationships, the person from Mars is dominating and can even be abusive but can also fight for others with unquenchable passion. What martian types need is to let go of the anger or anxiety that drives them and accept the eternal essences of their personalities that have been pushed aside by their fiery emotions.

The third circle shows the operation of Separation in which the black, earthbound Soul Bird splits into two white birds that retrieve the saved remains of Calcination and Dissolution. This is the first coming together of soul and spirit, and the newly acquired vantage point allows the discernment of what is worthy of being saved from the previous two operations. In psychological terms, the process of Separation retrieves the frozen energy released from the breaking down of habits and crystallized thoughts (assumptions, beliefs, and prejudices) and hardened feelings (emotional blockages, neuroses, and phobias). This misspent energy is now available to drive our spiritual transformation. Above this circle is the written *Terrae*, which means "of the Earth" and refers to the real or manifested essences being separated out from the dregs of matter at this stage.

Alchemical Separation is the rediscovery of our essence and the reclaiming of dream and visionary "gold" previously rejected by the masculine or rational part of our minds. It is, for the most part, a conscious process in which we review formerly unconscious material and decide what to discard and what to reintegrate into our personality. Much of this shadowy material consists of things we are ashamed of or have been taught to hide away by our parents, pastors, and teachers. Separation is letting go of the self-inflicted restraints to our true nature and saving the hidden essence, which becomes the subject of the following operations. That essence is made up of the best parts of our spirit and soul, our mind and heart. "The Wind carried it in its belly," says the tablet, and this stage is the first application of the Air Element in the Work. Separation delivers the retrieved spiritual essence safely through the processes of Calcination and Dissolution to its first incarnation, which is the earthly Conjunction.

Step 4: Conjunction (☿)

The fourth ray of the Azoth points to the area at the top of the drawing where the right wing of the Ascended Essence touches the salamander wallowing in flames. The ray is marked with the single symbol for both gold and the Sun and is often colored yellow or light green. The person with a golden temperament is courageous yet humble, full of spirit yet sensitive, and aware of the inner seed of radiance waiting to grow within everyone. This is the golden hue of the androgynous youth connected to both feeling and intellect. In relationships, the solar person tends to be very romantic and expects the same in return. In fact, the problem here is usually that the solar person is too idealistic and wants to stay anchored at this stage of development.

The fourth circle depicts the birds of soul and spirit leaving the earth together, lifting a five-spiked crown (the Fifth Element or Quintessence recovered from the preceding operations) into heaven or the realm of mind. This Conjunction is the turning point of the whole alchemical process and denotes the change from the forces of the *Anima* (Soul) in the triangle on the left to the forces of the *Spiritus* (Spirit) in the triangle on the right. Above this circle is inscribed the word *Rectificando*, which means "by rectification" or setting things right, and the wings of the Ascended Essence spread over this operation as if to bless it. On the personal level, Conjunction is the empowerment of our true selves, the union of both the masculine and feminine sides of our personalities into a new person who must still be nurtured to survive. The alchemists described this fragile child as a crude hermaphrodite, but as it grows in strength, the Child of the Philosophers solidifies into the Lesser Stone, a state of consciousness in which the adept is able to clearly discern what needs to be done to achieve permanent enlightenment.

The alchemists often referred to the Conjunction as the "Marriage of the Sun and Moon," which symbolized the two opposing ways of knowing or experiencing the world. Solar consciousness is intellectual and relies on rational thought; lunar consciousness is feeling based and taps into non-rational sources of information like psychic impressions and intuition. After this Marriage of the Mind, the initiate experiences an increase in intuitive insight that Egyptian alchemists called the birth of Intelligence of the Heart. This newly found faculty produces a sense of reality superior to either thought or feeling alone. As if to herald the viability of this new state of being, synchronicities begin to occur that confirm the alchemist is on the right track. The Conjunction can also be seen as the creation of an intuitive Overself that has perspective and insight into all realms of being — what Hermeticists would call a "thrice-greatest" person. In psychological terms, the Overself is the achievement of what Jungian psychologists call "individuation," in which the fragmented self is reunified into the original whole. Individuation can be seen as the melding of the personalities of the scientist with the artist or the businessman with the mystic. In simplest terms, it is the fusion of objective thought with our imaginative faculties. The birth of the Overself — the harmonious, whole person — means we have risen as far as we can on the earthly plane. "Its nurse is the Earth" is how the development of the Overself is described in the tablet, and it represents the first application of the Earth Element in the Work. At this point, the final goal of alchemy, the Greater Stone, is just starting to take shape.

Step Five: Fermentation (♆)

The fifth ray of the Azoth points to the area where the left wing of the Ascended Essence touches the standing bird of Spirit. The ray is marked with the cipher for the metal copper and the planet Venus. This section of the drawing is often colored turquoise or green, which is associated with the living energy of the Emerald Tablet, what the Sufis call the "Emerald Vision." The person with a cupric temperament is sanguine and ruled by the blood humor. This is the ray of the Spiritual Warrior, the person who has seen the way and wants to tell others of his or her discovery and to spread the vision of higher consciousness throughout the world. Relationships with people from Venus are as romantic as those from Mars but in a giving way and with greater substance to offer. For the venusian to make any progress, that special substance within has to be fermented from the powers Above, and a higher love must be achieved.

The fifth circle is under the inscription *Invenies*, which means "you will discover." This is the operation of Fermentation in which the unexpected mystic substance forms, the ambrosia of the gods, which represents the first lasting solidification of the conjoining of soul and spirit. The circled drawing shows the Soul and Spirit birds nesting in a tree, brooding over their egg, waiting for the mystical event to occur. Having achieved earthly balance and poise during the Conjunction, the alchemist looks Above for the next phase of his transformation. Fermentation is the introduction of new life into the product of Conjunction to completely change its characteristics, that is, to completely raise it to a new level of being. The tablet tells us to leave the earthly realm by the fire of imagination, "gently and with great Ingenuity," into a state that sets our soul afire with higher passion. This is the second or higher application of the Fire Element in the tablet, and the alchemists thought of it as working with the heavenly substance of Sulfur.

The overwhelming power from Above can take many forms. It can be a mystical experience, religious awakening, near-death experience, psychic vision, paranormal encounter, the achievement of grace in sports, or simply a winning attitude in business. Fermentation is achieved through a number of activities that include deep meditation, intense prayer, strong desire, breakdown of the personality, transpersonal therapy, activated imagination, continuous contemplation, or even the shamanic use of psychotropic drugs. In all cases, however, Fermentation is accomplished through what alchemists called the True Imagination, a state of consciousness in which mental images or visions seem more representative of reality than anything that we can see with our own eyes. It is as if our consciousness has left the bounds of matter and exists outside our bodies, and everything we experience in this state is more real and more truthful than the everyday world.

This transcendent phase is a true initiation of the personality into a new milieu that begins with the Putrefaction of the hermaphroditic child from the Conjunction resulting in its death Below in the world of illusion and its resurrection Above in the light of truth. This transcendent stage is far beyond the crowning psychological achievement of the Overself. The alchemical initiation, which is the Fermentation process, starts with the inspiration of spiritual power that reanimates, energizes, and enlightens the alchemist. The alchemist literally feels "on fire," but unlike the harsh fires of Calcination which attacked ego, the gentle warmth of Fermentation works on the spiritual child of the Conjunction just like a brooding hen sitting on its

eggs. The "hatching" of the new state of consciousness is often marked by a brilliant display of colors and meaningful visions called the "Peacock's Tail," which heralds the end of alchemy's tortuous Black Stage. Out of the blackness of the alchemist's personal Putrefaction comes the yellow Ferment, which "flows like a golden wax" in his brain. Chinese alchemists referred to this as the Golden Pill, which signifies the beginning of true enlightenment, the Yellow Stage of alchemy. This golden, waxy substance is the literal incarnation of higher thought. It is the product of our True Imagination becoming real. Fermentation is flooding the mind with meaningful and profoundly real images from something totally beyond us that lies at the edge of our personal reality. It is like a swinging door between one level of consciousness and another, between soul and spirit, between matter and mind.

Step Six: Distillation (△)

The Azoth's sixth ray points to the feather, symbol of Air and the process of spiritualization. This ray is associated with the color indigo or lapis blue with gold specks in it. It is marked with the symbol for the metal and planet Mercury, as well as an identical smaller symbol indicating the heavenly element of Mercury. A mercurial temperament means a flighty person, whose moods and behavior do not seem tied to any earthly explanation. Relationships with people from Mercury are always changing. Mercurians can be totally attentive and sensitive one minute and totally self-involved in the next. They need Distillation to fix their aspirations and gain perspective over their lives.

The sixth circle shows a unicorn lying on the ground in front of a rose bush. According to legend, the unicorn runs tirelessly from pursuers but lies meekly on the ground when approached by a virgin. In this case, the virgin is the purified alchemist, who has returned to a state of innocence through the release and purification of thoughts and emotions. Above the circle is the word *Occultum*, meaning secret or hidden. This circle represents the Distillation operation in which the purified soul will behold its object and peer into the eye of God. To do so demands the utmost purification which repeated distillations symbolize.

Chemically, Distillation is the boiling and condensation of the fermented solution to increase its purity, which is why this is known as the White

Stage of alchemy. Psychologically, this agitation and sublimation of psychic forces is necessary to ensure that no impurities from the lower personality are incorporated into the next and final process. "It rises from Earth to Heaven and descends again to Earth" is how the tablet describes Distillation, which represents the second or higher application of the Water Element in the tablet. The alchemists thought of this phase as working with the heavenly substance Mercury to extract and refashion the metals. The Ferment, the soft amalgam or balsam resulting from this operation must be hardened into a Stone before it can be made permanent, and the final phase of Distillation is a Sublimation in which vapor turns solid, or the spirit is made corporeal.

For the modern adept, Distillation consists of introspective techniques that attempt to raise the content of the psyche to the highest level possible, free from all sentimentality and personal attachments. Distillation takes us into the rarefied realm of the One Mind where base emotions cannot follow. It is the purification of the unborn Self — all that we truly are and can be spiritually.

Step Seven: Coagulation (♋)

The seventh ray of the Azoth points to the realm of the Queen and contains the symbol that stands for both the metal silver and the Moon. This ray is either colored purple, indicating royalty, or gray, representing silver and the Moon. The lunar or silver temperament is feminine and reflective, with a personality that tends to be volatile and manifested on multiple levels. In relationships with the lunar person, you end up doing most of the talking, but still waters run deep, and the lunar lover is sensuously supportive. The lunar type needs spiritual fulfillment and anchoring in a higher reality.

The final, seventh circle shows an androgynous youth emerging from an open grave, with the Latin word *Lapidem*, meaning "the Stone," next to it. This is the stage of Coagulation, in which the fermented Soul Child of the Conjunction is fused with the sublimated spiritual presence of Distillation. The resurrection of the soul is accomplished by bringing together only the purest essences of one's body and soul into the light of meditation. It becomes a permanent and always available state of consciousness that embodies the highest aspirations and evolution of mind and is sensed as a new strength of personality

to survive any onslaught. In the mystical sense, this "turning into Earth" is the realization of the eternal spirit body, often confirmed in an out-of-body experience.

The alchemists referred to this mobile state of consciousness as the Greater Stone, which is achieved first only in hypnagogic and semi-dream states but which eventually becomes solidified light that seems more real than our physical bodies. At that point, the alchemist has entered the final Red Stage and can use this wonderful presence to transform the reality of everything around him. The alchemists promised that from this Stone would flow the Red Elixir that heals all wounds and cures all diseases. In other words, Coagulation incarnates and releases the "Ultima Materia" of the soul that the Emerald Tablet described as the "Glory of the Whole Universe." Coagulation is the second or higher application of the elements Air and Earth in the tablet, and it results in a union of spirit with matter. At this stage, the alchemists felt they were working with the heavenly substance of Salt.

However, there is yet another, eighth step in our mandala. It is depicted in the Azoth drawing as the return to the first ray, the ray of Salt and Saturn that points to the Cubic Stone. For at the end of the alchemical process, we arrive back where we started from, only now empowered and embodied in an eternal Stone that represents an incorruptible higher consciousness.

There is also one last message hidden in the Azoth drawing. All the Latin words contained in the outer ring that connects the rays of transformation spell out a summary of what has taken place: *Visita Interiora Terrae Rectificando Invenies Occultum Lapidem.* This means "Visit the innermost parts of the earth; by setting things right ('rectifying'), you will find the hidden Stone." The first letter of these seven Latin words spells out "V-I-T-R-I-O-L." The highly corrosive Vitriol (sulfuric acid) is the liquid energy that drives chemical change and is likened to a brain ambrosia or hormone that brings on the transformation of the soul in humans.

Alchemical Correspondences

Operation	Associated Processes	Element Applied	Associated Metal	Chemical Arcanum	Process Colors	Process Odors
(1) Calcination	Roasting; Incineration; Dehydration; Pulverizing; Trituration	Fire △	Lead ♄ (Antimony ♁)	Sulfuric Acid (Vitriol)	Black; Magenta	Biting; Sulfuric; Brimstone
(2) Dissolution	Dissolving; Corrosion; Maceration; Cibation	Water ▽	Tin ♃	Iron Oxide (Rust)	Light blue; Pink	Acrid; Vinegary
(3) Separation	Sifting; Cutting; Fission; Extraction	Air △	Iron ♂	Sodium Carbonate (Soda Ash; *Natron carbonicum*)	Red	Rotten eggs
(4) Conjunction	Amalgamation; Conglomeration; Congelation; Reunion	Earth ▽	Copper ♀ (Gold ☉; Brass ♀)	Sodium Nitrate (Cubic Saltpeter; Fertile Salt; *Natron nitricum*)	Green	Chlorinic
(5) Fermentation	Digestion; Yeasting; Ceration	Sulfur	Mercury ☿ (Copper ♀)	Liquor Hepatis (Liquor of Soul)	Green-blue	Putrid and perfumed at same time
(6) Distillation	Exaltation; Circulation; Cohobation	Mercury ☿	Silver ☽ (Mercury ☿)	Black Pulvis Solaris (Black Powder of Spirit)	White; Rainbow	Fresh; After rain smell
(7) Coagulation	Fixation; Fusion; Sublimation; Projection; Multiplication	Salt ⊕	Gold ☉ (Silver ☽)	Red Pulvis Solaris (Red Powder of Spirit)	Violet; Purple	Flowery; Heavenly scented

(Note: Metals in parenthesis represent a Rosicrucian ordering popularized in the Renaissance.)

CHART 1: Correspondences of Chemical Characteristics

Operation	Planet	Day of Week	Planetary Influence	Zodiac	Numerology	Octave
(1) Calcination ▽	Saturn ♄	Saturday	Discipline; Limitation; Suppression of emotions	Aries ♈ (Calcination) Sagittarius ♐ (Incineration)	Monad	Do (C)
(2) Dissolution ♋	Jupiter ♃	Thursday	Expansion; Creation of Sociality; Incidences of Luck	Cancer ♋ (Solution)	Dyad	Re (D)
(3) Separation	Mars ♂	Tuesday	Assertiveness; Driving Energy	Scorpio ♏ (Separation)	Triad	Mi (E)
(4) Conjunction	Venus ♀ (Earth ⊕; Sun ☉)	Friday	Pleasure; Love; Freeing of emotions; Intuition	Taurus ♉ (Congelation)	Tetrad	Fa (F)
(5) Fermentation	Mercury ☿ (Venus ♀)	Wednesday	Encounter with the Divine Mind or Higher Energies	Leo ♌ (Digestion) Capricorn ♑ (Fermentation)	Pentad	So (G)
(6) Distillation	Moon ☽ (Mercury ☿)	Monday	Purification of instincts; Higher gnosis; Increased consciousness;	Virgo ♍ (Distillation) Libra ♎ (Sublimation)	Hexad	La (A)
(7) Coagulation ☍	Sun ☉ (Moon ☽)	Sunday	Vitality; Creativity; True Individuality; Realization of True Self in relationship to the Divine	Gemini ♊ (Fixation) Pisces ♓ (Projection) Aquarius ♒ (Multiplication)	Heptad	Ti (B)

(Note: Planets in parenthesis represent a Paracelsian ordering popularized in the Renaissance.)

CHART 2: Correspondences of Astronomical Bodies and the Music of the Spheres

Operation	Psychology	Conscious State	Intention/Desire	Negative Qualities	Positive Qualities
(1) Calcination	Ego; Purification of thoughts	Materialistic; Neurotic	Penitence; Maturity; Planning; Hope; Integration	Stubborn; Slow; Resigned; Passive; Cold; Fearful	Practical; Realistic; Patient; Prudent
(2) Dissolution	Id; Subconscious; Purification of feelings	Dreamy; Hypnagogic; Meditative	Beauty; Depth; Romance; Pleasure	Excessive; Greedy; Selfish love and sex; Inflated; Superficial	Generous; Sociable; Optimistic
(3) Separation	Essence; Ego centering; Purification of will	Mindful; Aware of opposites	Affluence, wealth; Courage; Power; Abundance; Health	Cruel; Violent; Angry; Abusive; Willful	Courageous; Daring; Initiating; Determined
(4) Conjunction	Essential union; Ego pairings; Purification of body; Integration of self	Blissful; In love; Enraptured	Fertility; Marriage; Homemaking; Personal presence	Lustful; Wanton; Possessive	Sensitive; Loving; Kind; Appreciative
(5) Fermentation	Inspiration; Religious fervor; Purification of soul; Soul Love + Will	Shamanistic consciousness; Beyond physical satisfaction	Wisdom; Intuition; Communication; Divine union	Tricky; Lying; Sneaky; Subjective	Hopeful; Lively; Imaginative; Creative
(6) Distillation	Divine Consciousness; Objectivity; Purification of spirit; Spirit Love + Will	Equanimity; One-pointedness; Point source of consciousness	Knowledge; Journey to Other Side; Psychic powers	Unemotional; Distanced; Detached	Intelligent; Reflective; Objective
(7) Coagulation	Transpersonal Self Divine Identity; the Stone; Purification of Self; Divine Love	Union with God; Nirvana; Satori; Synchronicities; Aware of non-self	Success; Illumination; Righteousness; Creative realization	Arrogant; Judgmental; Megalomania; Controlling	Confident; Intuitive; Authentic; Innocent; Whole

CHART 3: Correspondences of Psychology

Operation	Emerald Tablet	Yogic Path	Buddhism	Kabbalah	Church	Revelations
(1) Calcination	Its father is the Sun.	Yama (Abstention)	Asceticism; Concentration	Malkuth (Kingdom; Resplendence)	Ephesus	Seal of the White Horse
(2) Dissolution	Its mother the Moon.	Niyama (Self-improvement); Asana (Freeing bodily energy)	Access State; Meditation; the Jhanas	Yesod (Foundation; Innocence)	Laodicea	Seal of Silence
(3) Separation	The Wind carries it in its belly.	Pratyahara (Control of mind and senses)	Mindfulness; Basic Insight; Dukkha	Hod (Splendor; Perfection) Netzach (Victory; Power)	Pergam-os	Seal of the Red Horse
(4) Conjunction	Its nurse is the Earth.	Pranayama (Union of the two parts of the Life Force)	Pseudonirvana; Brilliant Lights; Rapture; Secret Chamber of the Heart; Presence	Tiphareth (Beauty; Meditation) Daath (Secret Knowledge of the Beyond)	Smyrna	Seal of the Black Horse
(5) Fermentation	Separate the Earth from Fire, the Subtle from the Gross.	Dharana (Fixing mind on object of devotion; concentration)	Realization of Higher Reality Avatar	Geburah (Severity; Justice) Chesed (Mercy; Receptiveness)	Thyatira	Seal of the Pale Horse
(6) Distillation	It rises from Earth to Heaven and descends again to Earth.	Dhyana (Meditation; undisturbed flow of thought)	Effortless Insight; Anatta, Anicca	Binah (Understanding; Sanctification) Chokmah (Wisdom; Illumination)	Philadel-phia	Seal of the Upheavals
(7) Coagulation	The Glory of the Whole Universe; the greatest Force of all powers.	Samadhi (Union with object of contemplation)	Nirodh; Beyond consciousness	Kether (Crown; Interdimensional)	Sardis	Seal of the Souls Slain

CHART 4: Correspondences of Spiritual Traditions

Operation	Mythological	Archangel	Images	Shamanism	Animal Totem
(1) Calcination	Set; Seth; Typhon; Amen; Atum; One Thing; Cronus; Saturn; Satan; Hephaestus (Vulcan)	Cassiel	Hellfire; Funeral Pyre; Cremation	Not Doing; Breaking the First Attention	Lizard; Bear; Crow
(2) Dissolution	Nephthys; Tefnut; Neptune; Rhea; Dionysus; Ishtar; Demeter	Sachiel	Floods; Melting; Tears; Intoxication; Sexual images	Stalking; Building Personal Power and Presence	Fish; Frog; Turtle
(3) Separation	Osiris; Shu; Geb and Nut; Apollo; Mars; Prometheus	Samael	Swords; Dismemberment; Divorce	Seeing; Cultivating the Second Attention	Owl; Beaver
(4) Conjunction	Isis; Athene; Sophia; Apis; Cupid (Eros); Zeus' wives; Venus; Aphrodite; Samson; Heracles (Hercules)	Anael	Glue, Chains; Sexual acts; Rosy Cross; Sacred Heart; Angels; UFO landings	Path of Heart; Leaving the Tonal World; Becoming a Spiritual Warrior	Deer; Buffalo; Bull
(5) Fermentation	Horus; Thoth; Hermes; Mercury; Odin; Christ; Krishna	Michael (Raphael)	Thunderstorms & Lightening; Grapes or wine barrels	Meeting the Ally; Entering the Nagual World	Snake; Rainbow Man; Wolf; Coyote
(6) Distillation	Ptah; Daedulus; Leda and Swan; Diana and Stag; Unicorn; Pegasus; Orpheus; Ganymedes; Jupiter	Gabriel	Dew; Rain; Baptismal fonts; Lotus flower	Death of Personal Desire; Creation of Clear Determination; Magical Will	Mountain Lion; White Buffalo
(7) Coagulation	Ra; the Aten; Solar Disk; One Mind; Amen-Ra; Apollo; Zeus	Raphael (Michael)	Wings; Gold; Stone or Egg; Embryo; Heaven	Impeccability; Perfect Projection; Shamanic Flight	Eagle

CHART 5: Correspondences of Myth and Imagination

Operation	Chakra	Physiological	Spectrum	Gemstone	Healing Effects
(1) Calcination ▽	Muladhara (Lead) Root Chakra (Physical; Instincts)	Sacrum; Seat; Tail bone; Anus; Eating food (metabolism)	Infrared; Darkest Red; Black; Lowest Frequency or Energy Level	Garnet; Red Jasper; Hematite; Obsidian	Courage; Strength; Grounding
(2) Dissolution	Svadhisthana (Tin) Genital Chakra (Sexuality; Sociality)	Genitals; Gonads Thighs; Spleen; Eating (drinking) water	Orange	Carnelian; Fire Opal	Warm energy; Fertility
(3) Separation	Manipura (Iron) Solar Plexus Chakra (Will; Intellect)	Solar plexus; Lungs and Diaphragm; Eating air; Gallbladder; Kidneys; Eating (absorbing) nutrients	Bright Yellow	Yellow Citrine; Tiger Eye; Ruby	Detoxification; Self-esteem; Uplifting; cheerful; Balance; Focus
(4) Conjunction	Anahata (Copper) Heart Chakra (Emotions; Feelings)	Heart; Blood; Eating (circulating) nutrients	Green	Emerald; Malachite; Jade; Aventurine; Kunzite; Rose Quartz	Strengthens heart/blood; Releases fear; Enhances dreams
(5) Fermentation	Vishuddha (Mercury) Throat Chakra (Concepts; Knowing; Communication)	Throat; Thymus; Thyroid; Limbic; Eating ideas and emotions	Turquoise; Light Blue	Turquoise; Blue Topaz; Aquamarine; Iolite; Clear Quartz	Balance nerves; align chakras; release creativity; begin channeling; vitalize energy
(6) Distillation	Ajna (Silver) Forehead Chakra (Intuition; Gnosis; Second Sight)	Brow; Pineal; Higher Heart; Liver, Seat of Soul; Eating images	Indigo; Deep Blue	Lapis Lazuli; Sodalite; Sapphire; Moldavite; Opal; Moonstone	Lymphatic; mental clarity; psychic powers
(7) Coagulation	Sahasrara (Gold) Crown Chakra (True Imagination)	Brain; Pituitary; Crown of head; Eating light	Violet; Ultraviolet; Highest Frequency or Energy Level	Amethyst; Pearl; Yellow Topaz; Flourite Crystal; Diamond	General healing; Regeneration

CHART 6: Correspondences of Bodily Energies

Operation	Tarot Lunar Conjunction	Tarot Solar Conjunction	Tarot Stellar Conjunction
(1) Calcination	(1) Magician (Mercury, Hermes, Thoth) Begin search for truth; conscious powers; realization of ego falsity; willpower; discipline to remove dross. Penetrating the Veil of the Profane; working the Cabalistic Left Pillar of Water and Severity Below.	(8) Strength (Hercules, Samson) Exaltation; strength of purpose; applied will; courage to proceed; self-confidence. Penetrating the Veil of Paroketh; working the Cabalistic Middle Pillar of Air and Mildness Between.	(15) Devil (Hermaphrodite, Typhon, Set) Fission; adversary; revealer of knowledge; seeing impurity to be eliminated to reunite. Penetrating the Veil of the Presence of the Ancient of Days; working the Right Pillar of Fire and Mercy Above.
(2) Dissolution	(2) High Priestess (Female Pope, Isis) Pure experience; unconscious powers; mystical union; lack of foresight.	(9) Hermit (Saturn) Meditation; time; wisdom; sage; withdrawal from society; self-absorption; slowing down to feel things.	(16) Tower (Athanor, Babel, Sodom) Higher dissolution; punishment of pride or ego; ruination of worldly approach.
(3) Separation	(3) Empress (Queen, Soul, Ishtar, Demeter) Fertility and birth; beauty; receptivity; recognizing essences; must do something.	(10) Wheel of Fortune (Midas) Overview of processes; change; eternal return; reincarnation; bad or good luck.	(17) Stars (Anahita, Aphrodite) Cosmic energy and perspective; new beginnings; salvation; faith; hope.
(4) Conjunction	(4) Emperor (King, Spirit, Dionysus) Ego stabilization; independence; active creativity; impregnation; power over illusion or status quo.	(11) Justice (Themis, Judge) Disposition; caution in taking advice; independent view, balance of ingredients; elimination of errors.	(18) Moon (Diana) *Hieros gamos,* uncertainty; changeability; open to powerful unseen influences; deception; cults; false Elixir.
(5) Fermentation	(5) Hierophant (High Priest, Pope, Zeus, Jupiter) Esoteric teachings; advice; healing; initiation; inspiration; conscience.	(12) Hanged Man (Christ, Odin) Death of ego; sacrifice of self; adaptability; higher purpose; release of essences for transformation.	(19) Sun (Apollo) Multiplication; health; wealth; gain; Projection; power; focused energy to those who succeed; true Elixir.
(6) Distillation	(6) Lovers (Cupid, Venus) Duality; recombination; choice; decision; gaining perspective on high level.	(13) Death (Orpheus) Complete mortification; wasted lives; transformation; rebirth; NDE.	(20) Judgement (God) Outside Wheel of Fortune; awakening; resurrection; one universal Life.
(7) Coagulation	(7) Chariot (Mars) Sublimation; achievement; control of opposing forces; victory; empowered.	(14) Temperance (Ganymede, Maria Prophetissa, Alchemist) Precipitation; mercy; moderation; service; conserving energy.	(21) World (Universe) Fusion; success; immortal presence; fulfillment; return to innocence; sex act in head; interdimensional.

CHART 7: Correspondences of the Tarot Tradition

(Note: Tarot Trump Cards 1-21 are archetypal energies in the Great Work; the 22nd card, the Fool or "0" card, is the subject of the journey.)

Made in the USA
Middletown, DE
08 July 2023